I love you because...

by
Marianne Richmond

I love you because...

Marianne Richmond Studios, Inc.
420 N. 5th Street, Suite 840
Minneapolis, MN 55401
www.mariannerichmond.com

ISBN 0-9741465-5-2

Illustrations by Marianne Richmond

Book design by Sara Dare Biscan

Printed in China

First Printing

TO Dan
FROM Nisa
Date 12/25/06

I love you because
you're you.

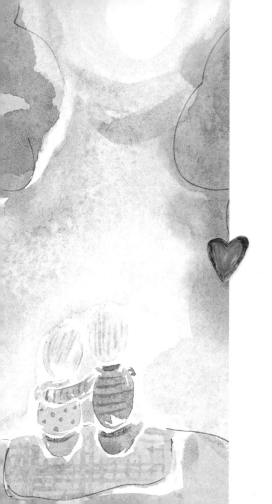

And I love
you and me
as us.

I'm so grateful that
   our paths crossed
along the way...
   and that we
shared the same
   crazy affection
for one another.
   I can't imagine
life without you.

I love you for
accepting the
various versions
of me.

Silly me.
Questioning me.
Whiny me.
Happy me.
Irrational (okay,
I admit it) me.

Female me.

I love you for
accepting that the
"drives-you-crazy"
me is just one
<u>itty</u> <u>bitty</u> part
of the greater,
lovable me.

I love you for the way you make
"everyday-ness"
more fun... our routines,
inside jokes and adventures.

I love you because you make me laugh. And you think I'm funny, too.

You do, don't you?

I love you for encouraging
me when I'm not feeling
very brave... or capable...
or successful.

You help me
see the positive,
and I need that.

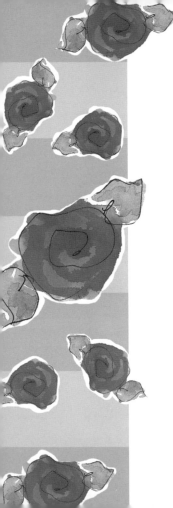

I love you
for trying to
understand a
woman's ways...

even when you
can't possibly
understand a
woman's ways.

I love you for
trying to
accept my need
for girl time,
frequent pampering,

numerous pairs of shoes,
and my recurrent urge to shop.

I love you for
saying you
like the change
to my hair...

even if you can't
really notice
the change to
my hair.

I love you for
your smile.

Your laughter, hugs
and kisses, too.

I love, love, love
each and every
inch of you!

I
love
cuddling
with
you.

I love you
for making
important to you
what's important
to me.

I know we don't <u>always</u> agree or get along. That would be a little unrealistic, don't you think? I love that we can voice our opinions... even get mad at each other... and still love each other through it.

I love being able
to co-exist with
you in the
same quiet space,
knowing we
don't have to
talk to enjoy
one another.

I love you because you
stretch yourself to
become a better person...
to learn more and
to love more.

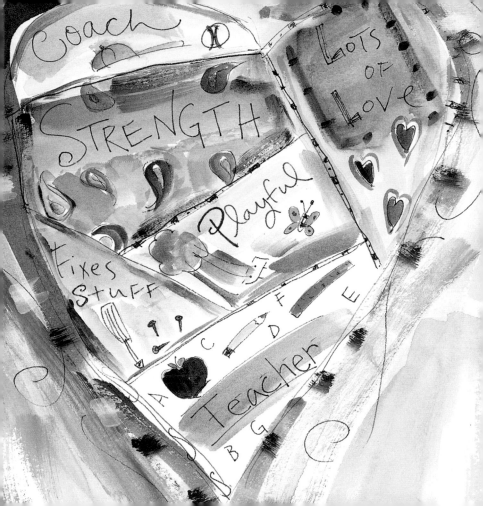

I love creating the story
of our love... knowing
each other long enough
to have history,
memories, dreams and genuine
concern for the
daily-ness of each other's life.

I love the thought of
journeying through this
crazy world together,
wherever it takes us.

I love you
because
you're my
life mate,
soul mate,
playmate
and friend.

My everything.
And my one
and only.

A gifted author and artist, Marianne Richmond shares
her creations with millions of people worldwide
through her delightful books, cards, and giftware.
In addition to the *Simply Said...* gift book series, she
has written and illustrated four additional books:
**The Gift of an Angel, The Gift of a Memory,
Hooray for You!** and **The Gifts of Being Grand.**

To learn more about Marianne's products, please visit
www.mariannerichmond.com.